U0111777

大展好書　好書大展
品嘗好書　冠群可期

大展好書　好書大展

品嘗好書　冠群可期

少林傳統功夫漢英對照系列

Shaolin Traditional Kungfu Series Boo

羅漢拳

Arhat Boxing

耿 軍 著

Written by Geng Jur

大展出版社有限

作者簡介

　　耿軍（法號釋德君），1968年11月出生於河南省孟州市，係少林寺三十一世皈依弟子。中國武術七段、全國十佳武術教練員、中國少林武術研究會副秘書長、焦作市政協十屆常委、濟南軍區特警部隊特邀武功總教練、洛陽師範學院客座教授、英才教育集團董事長。1989年創辦孟州少林武術院、2001年創辦英才雙語學校。先後獲得河南省優秀青年新聞人物、全國優秀武術教育家等榮譽稱號。

　　1983年拜在少林寺住持素喜法師和著名武僧素法大師門下學藝，成爲大師的關門弟子，後經素法大師引薦，又隨螳螂拳一代宗師李占元、金剛力功于憲華等大師學藝。在中國鄭州國際少林武術節、全國武林精英大賽、全國武術演武大會等比賽中6次獲得少林武術冠軍；在中華傳統武術精粹大賽中獲得了象徵少林武術最高榮譽的「達摩杯」一座。他主講示範的36集《少林傳統功夫》教學片已由人民體育音像出版社出版發行。他曾多次率團出訪海外，在國際武術界享有較高聲譽。

羅漢拳

　　他創辦的孟州少林武術院，現已發展成爲豫北地區最大的以學習文化爲主、以武術爲辦學特色的封閉式、寄宿制學校，是中國十大武術教育基地之一。

Brief Introduction to the Author

作者簡介

Geng Jun ﹝also named Shidejun in Buddhism﹞, born in Mengzhou City of Henan Province, November 1968, is a Bud–dhist disciple of the 31st generation, the 7th section of Chinese Wu shu, national "Shijia" Wu shu coach, Vice Secretary General of China Shaolin Wu shu Research Society, standing committee member of 10th Political Consultative Conference of Jiaozuo City, invited General Kungfu Coach of special police of Jinan Military District, visiting professor of Luoyang Normal University, and Board Chairman of Yingcai Education Group. In 1989, he estab–lished Mengzhou Shaolin Wu shu Institute; in 2001, he estab–lished Yingcai Bilingual School · He has been successively awarded honorable titles of "Excellent Youth News Celebrity of Henan Province" "State Excellent Wu shu Educationalist" etc.

In 1983, he learned Wu shu from Suxi Rabbi, the Abbot of Shaolin Temple, and Grandmaster Sufa, a famous Wu shu monk, and became the last disciple of the

Grandmaster. Then recom-mended by Grandmaster Sufa, he learned Wu shu from masters such as Li Zhanyuan, great master of mantis boxing, and Yu Xianhua who specializes in Jingangli gong. He won the Shaolin Wu shu champion for 6 times in China Zhengzhou International Wu shu Festival, National Competition of Wu lin Elites, National Wu shu Performance Conference, etc. and one "Damo Trophy" that symbolizes the highest honor of Shaolin Wu shu in Chinese Traditional Wu shu Succinct Competition. 36 volumes teaching VCD of Shaolin Traditional Wu shu has been published and is -sued by People's Sports Audio Visual Publishing House. He has led delegations to visit overseas for many times, enjoying high reputation in the martial art circle of the world.

Mengzhou Shaolin Wu shu Institute, established by him, has developed into the largest enclosed type boarding school of Yubei (north of Henan Province) area, which takes knowledge as primary and Wu shu as distinctiveness, also one of China's top ten Wu shu education bases.

序　言

中華武術源遠流長，門類繁多。

少林武術源自嵩山少林寺，因寺齊名，是我國拳系中著名的流派之一。少林寺自北魏太和十九年建寺以來，已有一千五百多年的歷史。而少林武術也決不是哪一人哪一僧所獨創，它是歷代僧俗歷經漫長的生活歷程，根據生活所需逐步豐富完善而成。

據少林寺志記載許多少林僧人在出家之前就精通武術或慕少林之名而來或迫於生計或看破紅塵等諸多原因削髮爲僧投奔少林，少林寺歷來倡武，並經常派武僧下山，雲遊四方尋師學藝。還請武林高手到寺，如宋朝的福居禪師曾邀集十八家武林名家到寺切磋技藝，推動了少林武術的發展，使少林武術得諸家之長。

本書作者自幼習武，師承素喜、素法和螳螂拳李占元等多位名家，當年如饑似渴在少林寺研習功夫，曾多次在國內外大賽中獲獎。創辦的孟州少林武術院亦是全國著名的武術院校之一，他示範主講的 36 集《少林傳統功夫》教學 VCD 已由人民體育音像出版社發行。

本套叢書的三十多個少林傳統套路和實戰技法是少

林武術的主要內容，部分還是作者獨到心得，很值得一讀，該書還採用漢英文對照，使外國愛好者無語言障礙，爲少林武術走向世界做出了自己的貢獻，亦是可喜可賀之事。

張耀庭題
甲申秋月

Preface

Chinese Wushu is originated from ancient time and has a long history, it has various styles.

Shaolin Wushu named from the Shaolin Temple of Songshan Mountain, it is one of the famous styles in the Chinese boxing genre. Shaolin temple has more than 1500 years of history since its establishment in the 19th year of North Wei Taihe Dynasty. No one genre of Shaolin Wushu is created solely by any person or monk, but completed gradually by Buddhist monks and common people from generation to generation through long–lasting living course according to the requirements of life. As recording of Record of Shaolin Temple, many Shaolin Buddhist monks had already got a mastery of Wushu before they became a Buddhist monk, they came to Shaolin for tonsure to be a Buddhist monk due to many reasons such as admiring for the name of Shaolin, or by force of life or seeing through thevanity of life. The Shaolin Temple always promotes Wushu and frequently appoints Wushu Buddhist monks to go down the mountain to roam around for searching masters and learning Wushu from them. It also invites

羅
漢
拳

Wushu experts to come to the temple, such as Buddhist monk Fuju of Song Dynasty, it once invited Wushu famous exports of 18 schools to come to the temple to make skill interchange, which promoted the development of Shaolin Wushu and made it absorb advantages of all other schools.

The author learned from many famous exports such as Suxi, Sufa and Li Zhanyuan of Mantis Boxing, he studied Chinese boxing eagerly in Shaolin Temple, and got lots of awards both at home and abroad, he also set up the Mengzhou Shaolin Wushu Institute, which is one of the most famous Wushu institutes around China. He makes demonstration and teaching in the 36 volumes teaching VCD of Shaolin Traditional Wushu, which have been published by Peoples sports Audio Visual publishing house.

There are more than 30 traditional Shaolin routines and practical techniques in this series of books, which are the main content of Shaolin Wushu, and part of which is the original things learned by the author, it is worthy of reading. The series books adopt Chinese and English versions, make foreign fans have no language barrier, and make contribution to Shaolin Wushu going to the world, which is delighting and congratulating thing.

Titled by Zhang Yaoting

目　錄
Contents

說　明

　　（一）為了表述清楚，以圖像和文字對動作作了分解說明，練習時應力求連貫銜接。

　　（二）在文字說明中，除特別說明外，不論先寫或後寫身體的某一部分，各運動部位都要求協調活動、連貫銜接，切勿先後割裂。

　　（三）動作方向轉變以人體為準，標明前後左右。

　　（四）圖上的線條是表明這一動作到下一動作經過的線路及部位。左手、左腳及左轉均為虛線（┈┈►）；右手、右腳及右轉均為實線（──►）。

Instructions

(i) In order to explain clearly figures and words are used to describe the actions in multi steps. Try to keep coherent when exercising.

(ii) In the word instruction, unless special instruction, each action part of the body shall act harmoniously and join coherently no matter it is written first or last, please do not separate the actions.

(iii) The action direction shall be turned taking body as standard, which is marked with front, back, left or right.

(iv) The line in the figure shows the route and position from this action to the next action. The left hand, left foot and turn left are all showed in broken line (--------►) ; the right hand, right foot and turn right are all showed in real line (——►) .

基本步型與基本手型
Basic stances and Basic hand forms

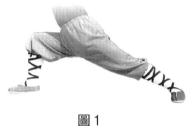

圖 1

圖 2

圖 3

圖 4

圖 5

圖 6

羅
漢
拳

圖 7

圖 8

圖 9

圖 10

圖 11

圖 12

基
本
步
型
與
基
本
手
型

圖 13

圖 14

圖 15

圖 16

圖 17

圖 18

圖 19

圖 20

圖 21

基本步型

少林武術中常見的步型有：弓步、馬步、仆步、虛步、歇步、坐盤步、丁步、併步、七星步、跪步、高虛步、翹腳步 12 種。

弓步：俗稱弓箭步。兩腿前後站立，兩腳相距本人腳長的 4～5 倍；前腿屈至大腿接近水平，腳尖微內扣不超過 5°；後腿伸膝挺直，腳掌內扣 45°。（圖 1）

馬步：俗稱騎馬步。兩腳開立，相距本人腳長的 3～3.5 倍，兩腳尖朝前；屈膝下蹲大腿接近水平，膝蓋與兩腳尖上下成一條線。（圖 2）

仆步：俗稱單叉，一腿屈膝全蹲，大腿貼緊小腿，膝微外展，另一腿直伸平仆接近地面，腳掌扣緊與小腿成 90°夾角。（圖 3）

虛步：又稱寒雞步。兩腳前後站立，前後相距本人腳長的 2 倍；重心移至後腿，後腿屈膝下蹲至大腿接近水平，腳掌外擺 45°；前腿腳尖點地，兩膝相距 10 公分。（圖 4）

歇步：兩腿左右交叉，靠近全蹲；前腳全腳掌著地，腳尖外展，後腳腳前掌著地，臀部微坐於後腿小腿上。（圖 5）

坐盤步：在歇步的形狀下，坐於地上，後腿的大小腿外側和腳背均著地。（圖 6）

丁步：兩腿併立，屈膝下蹲，大腿接近水平，一腳尖點地靠近另一腳內側腳窩處。（圖7）

併步：兩腿併立，屈膝下蹲，大腿接近水平。（圖8）

七星步：七星步是少林七星拳和大洪拳中獨有的步型。一腳內側腳窩內扣於另一腳腳尖，兩腿屈膝下蹲，接近水平。（圖9）

跪步：又稱小蹬山步。兩腳前後站立，相距本人腳長的2.5倍，前腿屈膝下蹲，後腿下跪，接近地面，後腳腳跟離地。（圖10）

高虛步：又稱高點步。兩腳前後站立，重心後移，後腿腳尖外擺45°，前腿腳尖點地，兩腳尖相距一腳距離。（圖11）

翹腳步：在七星螳螂拳中又稱七星步，兩腿前後站立，相距本人腳長的1.5倍，後腳尖外擺45°，屈膝下蹲，前腿直伸，腳跟著地，腳尖微內扣。（圖12）

基本手型

少林武術中常見的手型有拳、掌、鉤3種。

拳：

分為平拳和透心拳。

平拳：平拳是武術中較普遍的一種拳型，又稱方拳。四指屈向手心握緊，拇指橫屈扣緊食指。（圖

13）

　　透心拳：此拳主要用於打擊心窩處，故名。四指併攏捲握，中指突出拳面，拇指扣緊抵壓中指梢節處。（圖14）

　　掌：

　　分為柳葉掌、八字掌、虎爪掌、鷹爪掌、鉗指掌。

　　柳葉掌：四指併立，拇指內扣。（圖15）

　　八字掌：四指併立，拇指張開。（圖16）

　　虎爪掌：五指分開，彎曲如鉤，形同虎爪。（圖17）

　　鷹爪掌：又稱鎖喉手，拇指內扣，小指和無名指彎曲扣於掌心處，食指和中指分開內扣。（圖18）

　　鉗指掌：五指分開，掌心內含。（圖19）

　　鉤：

　　分為鉤手和螳螂鉤。

　　鉤手：屈腕，五指自然內合，指尖相攏。此鉤使用較廣，武術中提到的鉤均為此鉤。（圖20）

　　螳螂鉤：又稱螳螂爪，屈腕成腕部上凸，無名指、小指屈指內握，食指、中指內扣，拇指梢端按貼於食指中節。（圖21）

Basic stances

Usual stances in Shaolin Wushu are: bow stance, horse stance, crouch stance, empty stance, rest stance, cross – legged sitting, T – stance, feet – together stance, seven – star stance, kneel stance, high empty stance, and toes – raising stance, these twelve kinds.

Bow stance: commonly named bow – and – arrow stance. Two feet stand in tandem, the distance between two feet is about four or five times of length of one´s foot; the front leg bends to the extent of the thigh nearly horizontal with toes slightly turned inward by less than 5°; the back leg stretches straight with the sole turned inward by 45°. (Figure 1)

Horse stance: commonly named riding step. two feet stand apart, the distance between two feet is 3~3.5 times of length of one´s foot, with tiptoes turned forward; bend knees to squat downward, with thighs nearly horizontal, knees and two tiptoes in line. (Figure 2)

Crouch stance: commonly named single split. Bend the knee of one leg and squat entirely with thigh very close to lower leg and knee outspread slightly; straighten the other leg and crouch horizontally close to floor, keep the sole turned inward and forming an included angle of 90° with lower leg. (Figure 3)

Empty stance: also named cold – chicken stance. Two feet stand in tandem, the distance between two feet is 2 times of length of one´s foot; transfer the barycenter to back leg, bend the knee of the back leg and squat downward to the extent of the thigh nearly horizontal, with the sole turned outward by 45°; keep the tiptoe of front leg on the ground, with distance between two knees of 10cm. (Figure 4)

Rest stance: cross the two legs at left and right, keep them close and entirely squat; keep the whole sole of the front foot on the ground with tiptoes turned outward, the front sole of the back foot on the ground, and buttocks slightly seated on the lower leg of the back leg. (Figure 5)

Cross–legged sitting: in the posture of rest stance, sit on the ground, with the outer sides of the thigh and lower leg of the back leg and instep on the ground. (Figure 6)

T–stance: two legs stand with feet together, bend knees and squat to the extent of the thighs nearly horizontal, with one tiptoe on the ground and close to inner side of the fossa of the other foot. (Figure 7)

Feet –together stance: two legs stand with feet together, bend knees and squat to the extent of the thigh nearly horizontal. (Figure 8)

Seven–star stance: Seven–star step is a unique step form in Shaolin Seven –star Boxing and Major Flood Boxing. Keep the inner side of the fossa of one foot turned inward onto tiptoe of the other foot, bend two knees and squat nearly horizontal. (Figure 9)

Kneel stance: also named small mountaineering stance. Two feet stand in tandem, the distance between two feet is 2.5

times of length of one´s foot, bend knee of the front leg and squat, kneel the back leg close to the floor, with the heel of back foot off the floor. (Figure 10)

High empty stance: also named high point stance. Two feet stand in tandem. Transfer the barycenter backward, turn the tiptoe of the back leg outward by 45°, with tiptoe of front leg on the ground, and the distance between two tiptoes is length of one foot. (Figure 11)

Toes –raising stance: also named seven –star stance in Seven –star Mantis Boxing. Two legs stand in tandem, and the distance between two legs is 1.5 times of length of one´s foot. Keep the tiptoe of back leg turned outward by 45°, bend knees and squat, straighten the front leg with heel on the ground and tiptoe turned inward slightly. (Figure 12)

Basic hand forms

Usual hand forms in Shaolin Wushu are: fist, palm and hook, these three kinds.

Fist: classified into straight fist and heart–penetrating fist.

Flat fist: a rather common fist form in Wushu, also named square fist. Hold the four fingers tightly toward the palm, and horizontally bend the thumb to button up the fore finger. (Figure 13)

Heart –penetrating fist: mainly used for striking the heart part. Put four fingers together and coil –hold them, the middle finger thrusts out the striking surface of the fist, the thumb

buttons up and presses the end and joint of the middle finger.
(Figure 14)

Palm: classified into willow leaf palm, splay palm, tiger´s
claw palm, eagle´s claw palm, fingers clamping palm.

Willow leaf palm: palm with four fingers up and thumb
turned inward. (Figure 15)

Eight–shape palm: palm with four fingers up and thumb
splay. (Figure 16)

Tiger´s claw palm: palm with five fingers apart, bent as
hook and like tiger´s claw. (Figure 17)

Eagle´s claw palm: also named throat locking hand, with
the thumb turned inward, the little finger and middle finger
turned onto palm, fore finger and middle finger apart and turned
inward. (Figure 18)

Fingers clamp palm: palm with five fingers apart and palm
drawn in. (Figure 19)

Hook: classified into hook hand and mantis hook.

Hook hand: bend the wrist, five fingers drawn in naturally
with fingertips together. This hook is used in wide range, the
hook mentioned in Wushu refers to this. (Figure 20)

Mantis hook: also named mantis´ claw, bend wrist into
wrist bulge upward, the ring finger and little finger bend to hold
inward, with fore finger and fore middle finger turned inward
and end of thumb pressed on the middle joint of the fore finger.
(Figure 21)

羅漢拳套路簡介

Brief Introduction to the Routine Arhat Boxing

羅漢拳套路簡介

　　少林羅漢拳是少林寺優秀的傳統套路之一。本套路由 61 個動作組成，演練起來剛中含柔、柔中帶剛、剛柔相濟、發力疾快、招法連環，動作高低起伏、疾緩、動靜明顯，造型上有濃厚的佛教色彩，適合有一定武術基礎者演練。

Shaolin arhat boxing is one of excellent routines of traditional Shaolin Wushu. This routine consists of 61 movements. When performed or practised, it uses the temper force with grace, quick force exert, interlinked postures, with the actions heaving and setting, apparent quickness and slowness, keeping dynamic or static, and pattern with dense Buddhist color. It is suitable for the persons who has certain wushu base to perform or practise.

羅漢拳套路動作名稱
Action Names of Routine
Arhat Boxing

第一段　Section One

1. 預備勢　　Preparatory position
2. 羅漢拜佛　　Arhat worships Budda
3. 馬步雙分掌　　Separate palms in horse stance
4. 臥心拳　　Fist toward the heart
5. 羅漢捺虎　　Arhat restrains tiger
6. 羅漢抱印　　Arhat Hugs stamp
7. 摟手弓步沖拳　　Brush hand and thrust fist in bow stance
8. 彈腿沖拳　　Snap kick and thrust fist
9. 弓步沖拳　　Thrust fist in bow stance
10. 擰身歇步沖拳　　Twist body and thrust fist in rest stance
11. 馬步架打　　Parry and punch in horse stance
12. 砍掌踹腿　　Palm chop and side heel kick
13. 退步兩掌　　Step back and push palm twice
14. 丁步下栽拳　　Insert fist down in T-stance
15. 虎尾腳　　Tiger-tail foot

16. 劈腿　Leg split

17. 羅漢睡覺　Arhat sleeps

第二段　Section Two

18. 拉弓捶　Bow–pulling hammer

19. 金剛搗臼　Buddha´s warrior attendant pounds mortar

20. 羅漢蹲樁　Arhat squats as the stake

21. 獅子抖毛　Lion shakes hair

22. 黑虎掏心　Black tiger draws out heart

23. 提膝推掌　Lift knee and push palm

24. 鳳凰奪窩　Phoenix captures nest

25. 左右穿心肘　Left and right elbows pierce heart

26. 獨龍出洞　Single dragon comes out of cave

27. 追風炮　Cannon chasing the wind

28. 臥枕　Rest on the pillow

29. 端槍式　Holding gun position

30. 追蛇入洞　Chase the snake into cave

31. 虎尾腳　Tiger–tail foot

32. 二起腳　Jumping kick twice

33. 丁步亮掌　Flash palm in T–stance

第三段　Section Three

34. 龍盤窩　Dragon entrenches on cave

35. 仙人照鏡　Immortals looks into mirror

36. 迎面沙　Head-on sands

37. 分掌箭彈　Separate palms and thrust kick

38. 雙龍出洞　Two dragons come out of the cave

39. 坐蓮聽經　Listen to the sutra on the lotus seat

40. 羅漢托天　Arhat holds the sky

41. 羅漢下山　Arhat goes down the hill

42. 左右採腳　Slap left and right feet

43. 二起腳　Jumping kick twice

44. 雲頂　Cloud top

45. 七星　Seven star

46. 馬步單鞭　Single whip in horse stance

第四段　Section Four

47. 攔腰雙撅　Grasp waist for double punches

48. 小鬼提鞋　Ghost lifts shoe

49. 窩心肘　Elbow toward the heart

50. 反背捶　Backhand hammer

51. 連環五拳　Interlink five fists

52. 翻身連珠炮　Cannons in succession
　　　　　　　　with turning-over

53. 回身兩拳　Turn body and punch twice

54. 羅漢步雲　Arhat steps on the cloud

55. 擊地炮　Ground cannon

56. 雲頂　Cloud top

57. 七星　Seven star

58. 馬步單鞭　Single whip in horse stance

59. 二起腳　Jumping kick twice

60. 五花坐山　Swing arms with horse stance

61. 收勢　Closing form

羅漢拳套路動作圖解
Action Illustrtion of Routine Arhat Boxing

圖 1

第一段　Section One

1. 預備勢　Preparatory position

(1)兩腳併立；兩手自然下垂，五指併攏，貼於體側；目視前方。（圖 1）

(1) Stand upright with feet together, two hands drop naturally, five fingers put to gether and keep close to the side of the body respectively. Eyes look forward.〔Figure 1〕

圖 2

(2)左腳向身體左側橫跨半步；同時，兩手上提變拳，抱於兩腰間；目視左方。（圖2）

要點：身體正立，挺胸塌腰，頭正頸直，挺胸收腹，抱拳迅速。

(2) The left foot strides a half–step horizontally to the left, at the same time two hands lift upward and change into fists, then hold on the waist. Eyes look leftward.（Figure 2）

Key points: the body stands up, with chest lifting and waist down–ward, head being correctitude and neck straight. Lift the chest, draw in the abdomen and hold fists quickly.

圖 3

2. 羅漢拜佛　Arhat worships Budda

　　（1）接上勢。兩拳變掌，掌心向下，由身體兩側向上畫掌，至與肩同高時，兩掌上翻為掌心向上，然後繼續畫至頭頂，掌心相對，掌指向上；目視上方。（圖3）

　　(1) Follow the above posture, change two fists into palms with the palms downward, swing palms upward from the both sides of the body at the shoulders level, two palms turn up with the palms up, then continue to swing to the head top, with the palms opposite and the fingers up. Eyes look forward.〔Figure 3〕

圖 4

（2）上動不停。右腿獨立，左腿收回，左腳踝放於右膝蓋上；同時，向下蹲身；雙掌合十，自頭頂下落於胸前；目視前方。（圖4）

(2) Don´t stop the above action, the right leg stands alone and draw back the left one, and the left ankle puts on the right knee. At the same time, squat the body; bring two palms together and lower to the front of chest from the head top. Eyes look forward.〔Figure 4〕

圖 5

3. 馬步雙分掌
Separate palms in horse stance

接上勢。左腿向左側落地成馬步;同時,兩掌內翻,使掌心朝向面部,然後兩掌再外翻,向身體兩側分掌平推;目視左掌。(圖 5)

Follow the above posture, the left leg falls to the ground leftward and change into the horse stance. At the same time, two palms turn inward, with the palms toward the face, then turn two palms outward, separate palms for horizontal push toward the both sides of the body. Eyes look at the left palm.(Figure 5)

羅漢拳套路動作圖解

圖6

4. 臥心拳 Fist toward the heart

(1)接上勢。身體左轉 90°，重心前移成左弓步；同時，左臂外旋微屈，左手抓握成拳，拳心朝上，拳眼朝左，高與肩平；右掌變拳抱於右腰間，拳心朝上。（圖 6）

(1) Follow the above posture, turn the body 90° to the left, shift the barycenter forward and change into the left bow stance. At the same time, whirl the left arm outward and bend it slightly. Clench the left hand and change into the fist with the fist－palm up, the fist－hole leftward and at the shoulder level. Change the right palm into fist and put on the right waist with the fist－palm up.（Figure 6）

羅
漢
拳

圖 7

(2)上動不停。右腳向前上步，震腳成蹲步；同時，左拳屈臂回收；右拳經左前臂內側向前上方抄拳，拳心向裏，高與肩平；左拳拳心貼於右肘外側，拳眼斜向上；發「嗯」聲，目視前方。（圖7）

(2) Don´t stop the above action, the right foot steps forward, stamp foot into the squat stance. At the same time, bend the arm to draw back the left fist while lifting the right fist upward through the inner side of the left arm with the fist−palm inward at the shoulder level. Close the left fist−palm to the outer side of the right elbow with the fist −hole upward aslant. Make the sound of "en" and eyes look forward.（Figure 7）

羅漢拳套路動作圖解

圖 8

5. 羅漢捺虎　Arhat restrains tiger

(1)接上勢。身體起立，右腿抬起，向前彈腿踢出；同時，右拳收回腰間；左拳變掌，向前橫掌推出，高與肩平；目視左掌。（圖 8）

(1) Follow the above posture, the body stands up, lift the right leg, do snap kick forward. At the same time, draw back the right fist on the waist; change the left fist into palm and push forward with horizontal palm at the shoulder height. Eyes look at the left palm.（Figure 8）

圖9

(2)上動不停。左腳小跳，右腳落地，屈膝下蹲，左腳向左側鏟出，平仆成左仆步；同時，右拳變掌，兩掌內翻，經胸前下按拍擊地面，兩掌十指尖相對，身體略前俯；目視兩掌指尖。（圖9）

(2) Keep the above action, the left foot jumps slightly, the right foot lands to the ground, and bend knee for squatting down, the left foot shovels out leftward, and crouch forward into the left crouch stance. At the same time, change the right fist into palm, two palms turn inward, press down and slap the ground through the front of the chest, with ten finger tips of two palms opposite. The body bows forward lightly and eyes look at the finger tips of two palms. ﹝Figure 9﹞

圖 10

6. 羅漢抱印　Arhat Hugs stamp

（1）接上勢。重心左移成馬步；同時，右掌向後回環畫弧，屈臂收於胸前，掌心朝下；左掌向前畫弧內翻，屈臂上提，成掌心朝上；右掌在左臂肘上方，左掌在右臂肘下方；目視右掌指。（圖 10）

(1) Follow the above posture, shift the barycenter leftward into the horse stance. At the same time, turn the right palm backward and pull an arc, bend the arm and draw back in front of the chest with the palm down; the left palm pulls an arc forward and turns inward, bend the arm and lift it with the palm up. Put the right palm above the elbow of the left arm while the left palm under the elbow of the right arm. Eyes look at the fingers of the right palm. (Figure 10)

圖 11

　　(2)上動不停。右腳向左腳內側併步，身體起立；同時，兩肘向身體兩側分拉橫擊，兩掌掌心在胸前上下相對；目視左側。（圖 11）

　　(2) Don´t stop the above action, move the right foot toward the inner side of the left foot, and the body stands up. At the same time, pull the two elbows toward the both sides of the body for the horizontal punch. The two palms are opposite up and down in front of the chest. Eyes look at the left side.（Figure 11）

圖 12

7. 摟手弓步沖拳

Brush hand and thrust fist in bow stance

接上勢。身體左轉 90°，左腳向前上一步成左弓步；左掌外摟變拳回抱腰間；右掌變拳，隨身體左轉之勢，自右腰間向前方沖出；目視右拳。（圖 12）

Follow the above posture, the body turns 90° to the left. The left foot takes a step forward to make a left bow stance, the left palm grabs outward, then change it into fist and hold on the waist. Change the right palm into fist, and punch forward from the waist with the body turning to the left. Eyes look at the right fist.（Figure 12）

羅
漢
拳

圖 13

8. 彈腿沖拳　Snap kick and thrust fist

接上勢。重心前移，左腿直立，右腿向前彈踢；
同時，右拳屈臂收回腰間，拳心朝上；左臂內旋，左
拳向前方沖拳，高與肩平；目視左拳。（圖 13）

Follow the above posture, shift the barycenter forward,
straighten the left leg, the right leg does the snap kick forward.
At the same time, bend the arm and draw back the right fist on
the waist with the fist –palm up; rotate the left arm inward, the
left fist punches forward, at the shoulder height. Eyes look at the
left fist.（Figure 13）

羅漢拳套路動作圖解

圖 14

9. 弓步沖拳　Thrust fist in bow stance

接上勢。右腳向後下落，成左弓步；同時，左拳收回腰間，拳心向上；右拳向前沖拳，拳心向下，高與肩平；目視右拳。（圖 14）

Follow the above posture, the right foot lands down backward into the left bow stance. At the same time, draw back the left fist on the waist with the fist –palm up; the right fist punches forward with the fist –palm downward at the shoulder height. Eyes look at the right fist.（Figure 14）

圖 15

10. 擰身歇步沖拳

Twist body and thrust fist in rest stance

　　(1)接上勢。上身姿勢不變；左腳略回收，以右腳跟為軸，右轉身 270°；右拳直臂隨轉身平擺；兩腿成交叉步；目視前方。（圖 15、圖 15 附圖）。

羅漢拳套路動作圖解

圖 15 附圖

(1) Follow the above posture, keep the posture of the upper body unchangeable. Draw back the left foot slightly and the body turns 270° to the right with the right heel as the pivot. Erect the arm, swing the right fist horizontally with the rotation of the body. Change two legs into the cross stance. Eyes look forward. (Figure 15, Attached figure 15)

圖 16

(2)上動不停。身體下蹲成歇步；同時，左拳向前平沖，高與肩平；右拳收回腰間；目視左拳。（圖16、圖16附圖）

要點：擰身輕靈快捷，沖拳迅猛有力，力達拳面。

圖 16 附圖

(2)Don´t stop the above action, the body squats downward into the rest stance. At the same time, the left fist punches forward horizontally at the shoulder level; draw back the right fist on the waist. Eyes look at the left fist. (Figure 16, Attached figure 16)

Key points: twist the body lightly, smartly and quickly, strike forward rapidly and forcefully with the force reaching the fist-plane.

圖 17

11. 馬步架打
Parry and punch in horse stance

(1)接上勢。身體起立，左腿提起，左腳扣於右膝後；同時，左拳收回腰間；右拳變掌，經胸前向左側砍掌，高與胯平；目視右掌。（圖 17）

(1) Follow the above posture, the body stands up, lift the left leg and the left foot pressed behind the back of the right knee. At the same time, draw back the left fist on the waist; change the right fist into palm and chop leftward through the front of the chest at the hip level. Eyes look at the right palm.〔Figure 17〕

圖 18

(2)上動不停。左腳向左側落步成馬步；同時，右掌翻掌上架於頭前上方；目視左拳。（圖 18）

(2) Don´t stop the above action, the left foot lands leftward into the horse stance. At the same time, turn the right palm to raise over the front of the head. Eyes look at the left fist.（Figure 18）

羅漢拳

圖 19

12. 砍掌踹腿　Palm chop and side heel kick

(1)接上勢。身體提起，左轉身 180°；同時，右掌掄臂向前砍掌，掌心向上，掌指向前，略高於肩；左拳屈臂回收於右腋下，拳心向下；目視右掌。（圖19）

(1) Follow the above posture, uplift the body and turn it 180° to the left. At the same time, swing the arm and the right palm chops forward with the palm up and the fingers forward, higher than the shoulder slightly; bend the arm and draw back the left fist under the right armpit with the fist–palm downward. Eyes look at the right palm.（Figure 19）

圖 20

（2）上動不停。抬右腳向右側踹腿；同時，左肘後拉，左拳置於左肩前，拳心向下；右掌屈臂收回，隨即翻掌向右側推出，掌心向右，高與眼平；目視右腳。（圖20）

(2) Don´t stop the above action, lift the right foot for the side heel kick rightward. At the same time, pull back the left elbow, put the left fist before the left shoulder with the fist–palm down; bend the arm and draw back the right palm, then turn the palm and push it rightward at once with palm rightward at eye level. Eyes look at the right foot.（Figure 20）

圖 21

13. 退步兩掌
Step back and push palm twice

(1) 接上勢。右腳下落，身體左轉 90°；同時，左拳收回腰間，拳心向上；右掌向前方平推，掌指向上，高與肩平；目視右掌。（圖 21）

(1) Follow the above posture, the right foot fall down and the body turns 90° to the left. At the same time, draw back the left fist on the waist with the fist–palm upward; push the right palm forward horizontally with the fingers of the palm upward at the shoulder height. Eyes look at the right palm.（Figure 21）

圖 22

(2)上動不停。左腳向後退一步，腳尖點地成交叉
步；同時，右掌收回腰間，拳心向上；左拳變掌向前
平推，掌指向上，高與肩平；目視左掌指。（圖 22）

(2) Don´t stop the above action, the left foot takes a step
backward with the tiptoe on the ground to become the cross
stance. At the same time, draw back the right palm on the waist
with the fist–palm up; change the left fist into palm for the
horizontal push forward with the fingers of the palm upward at
the shoulder level. Eyes look at the fingers of the left palm.
（Figure 22）

圖 23

14. 丁步下栽拳
Insert fist down in T-stance

　　(1) 接上勢。右腳向後撤一步，身體右轉 180°；同時，右掌從身體右側向上、向後畫圓，變拳收於右腰間，拳心向上；左掌屈臂回收，經胸前向下、向外畫一大圓，橫掌下按於胸前，掌指向右，高與肩平；目視左掌。（圖 23）

羅漢拳套路動作圖解

(1) Follow the above posture, the right foot takes a step backward and the body turns 180° to the right. At the same time, the right palm pulls a circle upward and backward from the right side of the body, then change it into fist and draw back it on the waist with the fist–palm up; bend the arm and draw back the left palm, pull a big circle downward and outward through the front of the chest, make the palm horizontal and press downward before the chest with the fingers rightward at the shoulder level. Eyes look at the left palm. (Figure 23)

圖 24

(2) 上動不停。左腳向右腳內側上步，蹲身成左丁步；同時，左掌變拳收抱於腰間，拳心向上；右拳向前下方沖拳，拳面朝斜下方；目視右拳。（圖 24）

(2) Don´t stop the above action, the left foot steps toward the inner side of the right foot and squat the body into the left T-stance. At the same time, change the left palm into fist and draw it back on the waist with the fist-palm upward; the right fist strikes ahead downward with the fist-plane downward aslant. Eyes look at the right fist.（Figure 24）

圖 25

15. 虎尾腳 Tiger-tail foot

接上勢。右拳收回腰間,拳心向上;同時,身體微左轉,左腳提起向左側上方踹腿;目視左腳。(圖25)

要點:踹腿迅速有力,力達腳跟。

Follow the above posture, draw back the right fist on the waist with the fist-palm upward. At the same time, turn the body to the left slightly; raise the left foot for the side heel kick toward the left ahead. Eyes look at the left foot. (Figure 25)

Key points: kick quickly and forcefully with the force reaching the heel.

圖 26

16. 劈腿　Leg split

(1)接上勢。身體右轉 90°，左腳向右腳前方落步；同時，兩臂屈肘上抬，成兩肘尖向外，兩拳置於兩耳側，拳面相對，高與耳平；目視前方。（圖 26）

(1) Follow the above posture, turn the body 90° to the right, the left foot lands to ahead of the right one. At the same time, bend the elbows to lift the arms with the tips of elbows outward, place the fists on sides of ears with the fist-planes opposite at the ear level. Eyes look forwards.（Figure 26）

圖 27

（2）上動不停。右腳向前方正踢腿；同時，右拳直臂下劈於體右側；左拳收回抱於腰間；目視右腳尖。（圖 27 ）

要點：踢腿要高，右腳腳尖回勾。

(2) Don´t stop the above action, the right foot kicks right ahead. At the same time, the right fist with straight arm hacks to the right side of the body, draw back the left fist on the waist. Eyes look at the right tiptoe.（Figure 27 ）

Key points: the leg shall kick highly, hook the right tiptoe back.

圖 28

17.羅漢睡覺　Arhat sleeps

(1)接上勢。右腳落於左腳前方，隨即左腳向前上一步，右腳尖離地成交叉步；同時，右臂向上、向前掄臂；左臂向後、向上掄臂；兩臂右前左後成水平，兩掌心向下；目視前方。（圖28）

(1) Follow the above posture, the right foot lands before the left one, then the left foot takes a step forward, keep the right tiptoe lift off in the cross stance. At the same time, swing the right arm upward and forward; swing the left one backward and upward. The arms in the right to front and left to back shall be horizontal with the palms down. Eyes look forward.（Figure 28）

圖 29

（2）上動不停。身體下蹲成坐盤步；同時，左手經胸前變拳下栽，拳面抵於右腳踝上；右掌屈臂回收，經胸前向上抄拳，右肘支撐於左腳面；身體稍向右傾，頭枕於右拳面；目視左方。（圖 29）

(2)Don´t stop the above action, squat the body into a cross-legged sitting. At the same time, change the left hand into fist to punch downward through the front of the chest, press the fist-plane on the right ankle; bend the arm to draw back the right palm, lift the fist upward through the front of the chest, the right elbow presses on the left instep; the body slants rightward and the head on the right fist-plane. Eyes look leftward. (Figure 29)

圖 30

第二段　Section Two

18. 拉弓捶　Bow-pulling hammer

　　接上勢。身體起立，右轉 180°成馬步；同時，右肘向身體右側橫拉，高與肩平，右拳置於右肩前，拳心向下；左拳經胸前向左沖拳，拳心向下，高與肩平，力達拳面；目視左拳。（圖 30）

羅漢拳套路動作圖解

Follow the above posture, the body stands up and turns 180° to the right into the horse stance. At the same time, horizontally pull the right elbow toward the right side of the body, at the shoulder level, and put the right fist in front of the right shoulder with the fist–palm down; the left fist strikes leftward through the front of the chest with the fist–palm downward at the shoulder height, the force reaching the fist –plane. Eyes look at the left fist. (Figure 30)

羅
漢
拳

圖 31

19. 金剛搗臼
　　Buddha's warrior attendant pounds mortar

　　(1) 接上勢。身體右轉 90°，隨即向左轉 180°成跪步；同時，左拳變掌，隨身體轉動在身體左側由下向上畫一圓弧，擺向身體左後方，掌心向後，掌指向下；右拳抱於腰間，隨即右臂下垂，右拳向前擺於左腿前，拳面向下，拳眼向左；目視右拳。（圖 31）

羅漢拳套路動作圖解

(1) Follow the above posture, the body turns 90° to the right, then turns 180° to the left into the kneel stance at once. At the same time, change the left fist into palm and pull a circular arc downward to upward at the left side of the body with the rotation of the body, swing to the left back of the body with the palm backward and the fingers downward; hold the right fist on the waist, then drop down the right arm immediately, make the right fist forward and put it in front of the left leg with the fist–palm downward and the fist–hole leftward. Eyes look at the right fist.
(Figure 31)

圖 32

　　(2) 上動不停。左腳獨立，右腿屈膝提起，高與胯平，腳尖內扣；同時，右臂屈肘上提，前臂略高於肩，拳心向外，拳眼向下；左掌內翻成掌心向斜前方，掌指向下；目視前方。（圖 32、圖 32 附圖）

罗汉拳套路动作图解

圖 32 附圖

(2)Don´t stop the above action, the left foot stands alone, bend the knee of the right leg and lift it at the hip level, and tiptoe turns inward. At the same time, bend the elbow of the right arm and uplift it, keep the lower part of the arm higher than the shoulder slightly, with the fist−palm outward and the fist−hole down. Turn the left palm inward into the palm forward aslant and the fingers down. Eyes look forward. (Figure 32, Attached figure 32)

圖 33

(3) 上動不停。右腳震腳，落於左腳內側，重心下移成蹲步；同時，左掌屈臂向腹前抄起；右拳外翻，拳背向下砸於左掌心；目視右拳。（圖 33、圖 33 附圖）

要點：轉身、掄臂要協調一致；蹲步時大腿接近水平；震腳與砸拳要同時完成，迅速有力。

羅漢拳套路動作圖解

圖 33 附圖

(3) Don't stop the above action, stamp the right foot and land at the inner side of the left foot, lower the barycenter into the squat stance. At the same time, bend the arm and lift the left palm toward the front of the abdomen; turn the right fist outward with the back of the fist down and pounding at the left palm. Eyes look at the right fist. (Figure 33, Attached figure 33)

Key points: harmonize the body turn with the arm swing; In the squat stance, the thigh shall be close to the horizontal; stamping foot and pounding fist shall simultaneously be completed rapidly and forcefully.

圖 34

20. 羅漢蹲樁
Arhat squats as the stake

　　接上勢。身體起立，左腳向左側橫跨一步，身體
下蹲成馬步；同時，左掌變拳，兩拳向外、向上環
繞，經胸前向下栽拳，兩臂屈肘，拳面抵於兩膝蓋
上，拳心向後，拳眼相對；目視左方。（圖34）

羅
漢
拳
套
路
動
作
圖
解

Follow the above posture, the body stands up, the left foot strides a step leftward, the body squats to become the horse stance. At the same time, change the left palm into fist, two fists circle outward and upward. Punch downward through the front of the chest, bend elbows of two arms, the fist–planes prop on the two knees, with the fist–palm backward, the fist–hole opposite. Eyes look leftward. (Figure 34)

羅
漢
拳

圖 35

21. 獅子抖毛
Lion shakes hair

(1) 接上勢。右腳蹬地跳起，向左落於左腳處，隨即左腳小跳，左膝抬起；同時，右臂直臂由外向內、向前擺動，拳心朝上，略低於肩；左臂屈肘收回腰間，拳心朝上；目視前方。（圖 35）

羅漢拳套路動作圖解

(1) Follow the above posture, the right foot jumps up from the ground, land at the part of the left foot leftward, then the left foot makes a small jump immediately, and lift the left knee. At the same time, swing the stretched right arm inward and forward from outward, with the fist–palm up, lower than the shoulder; bend elbow of the left arm and draw it back on the waist with the fist–palm up. Eyes look forward. (Figure 35)

圖36

(2) 上動不停。左腳向左側落步，向下蹲身成馬步；同時，右臂屈肘，向身後頂肘，左臂微屈，向前自然擺動，拳心向上；目視左拳。（圖36）

(2) Do not stop the above action, left foot lands leftward, squat the body downward to become the horse stance. At the same time, bend the right elbow and strike it toward the back of the body, bend the left arm slightly and naturally swing forward, with the fist–palm up. Eyes look at the left fist.〔Figure 36〕

圖 37

(3) 上動不停。左臂屈肘，向身後頂肘，右臂微
屈，向前自然擺動，拳心向上；目視右拳。（圖 37）

(3) Do not stop the above action, bend elbow of the left arm
to strike toward the back of the body, bend the right arm slightly
and naturally swing forward, with the fist–palm up. Eyes look at
the right fist.（Figure 37）

圖 38

(4) 上動不停。右臂屈肘，向身後頂肘，左臂微屈，向前自然擺動，拳心向上；目視左拳。（圖 38）

(4) Do not stop the above action, bend elbow of the right arm to strike toward the back of the body, bend the left arm slightly and naturally swing forward, with the fist-palm up. Eyes look at the left fist.〔Figure 38〕

圖 39

22. 黑虎掏心 Black tiger draws out heart

接上勢。身體左轉 90°，雙腳跳起互換位置，重心前移至右腿，成右弓步；同時，左拳收抱於腰間；右拳從後向胸前抄拳，右臂微屈，拳心朝裏，高與頜平；目視右拳。（圖 39）

Follow the above posture, the body turns 90° to the left, two feet jump up and interchange positions, shift barycenter forward to the right leg and change into bow stance. At the same time, draw back the left fist and hold it on the waist; uppercut with the right fist from the back to the front of the chest, bend the right arm slightly, with the fist–palm inward, high with the jaw. Eyes look at the right fist.（Figure 39）

圖 40

23. 提膝推掌　Lift knee and push palm

接上勢。以右腳為軸，身體左轉 180°，右腳獨立，左腳提起，腳尖內扣繃直；同時，右拳變掌自右腰間向前立掌推出，掌心向前，高與肩平；左拳屈臂回拉至左肩前，拳眼朝裏，拳心朝下；目視右掌。（圖 40、圖 40 附圖）

要點：轉身迅速，獨立穩固，左大腿高與胯平，左右臂在同一水平。

圖 40 附圖

Follow the above posture, the body turns 180° to the left with the right foot as the pivot, the right foot stands alone and lift the left one, tiptoe turns inward and stretchs tight. At the same time, change the right fist into palm and push out with standing palm from the right waist to forward, with palm forward, high with the shoulder, bend arm and pull the left fist back to the front of the left shoulder, with the fist-hole inward, the fist-palm down. Eyes look at the right palm. ﹝Figure 40, Attached figure 40﹞

Key points: turn around quickly, stand alone steady, keep the left thigh high with the hip, and two arms at the same level.

圖 41

24. 鳳凰奪窩　Phoenix captures nest

（1）接上勢。左腳落於右腳左前方；同時，右掌變拳向後擺，拳心向下，略低於肩；左拳變掌，左臂伸直前擺，掌心向上，高與肩平，兩臂在同一水平；目視前方。（圖 41）

（1）Follow the above posture, the left foot lands at the left front of the right foot. At the same time, change the right palm into fist to swing backward, with the fist-palm down, lower than the shoulder slightly; change the left fist into palm, stretch the left arm straightly and swing forward, with the palm up, high with the shoulder, two arms at the same level. Eyes look forward.（Figure 41）

羅漢拳套路動作圖解

圖 42

（2）上動不停。右腳經左腿內側以腳跟擦地向前搓踢，腳尖向右上方；同時，右拳經體側由後向前、向上挑臂外格肘；左掌經胸前下按置於右肘內側，掌心向下，掌指向右；目視前方。（圖 42）

（2）Don't stop the above action, the right foot shuffles forward with the heel through the inner side of the left leg, tiptoe turns right upward. At the same time, lift the outside elbow of the arm with the right fist through the side of the body from backward to forward and upward; press the left palm through the front of the chest and put it at the inner side of the right elbow, with the palm down, the fingers rightward. Eyes look forward.
（Figure 42）

圖 43

25. 左右穿心肘
Left and right elbows pierce heart

(1) 接上勢。重心前移，右腳向前落步；同時，左掌變拳，兩拳分別從胸前經身體兩側向後擺拳，置於臀後方，兩拳心相對，拳眼斜向下；目視前方。（圖43）

羅漢拳套路動作圖解

(1) Follow the above posture, shift the barycenter forward, the right foot lands forward. At the same time, change the left palm into fist, swing two fists backward through two sides of the body in front of the chest respectively, put them at the back of the buttocks, with two fist-palms opposite, fist-holes down aslant. Eyes look forward. (Figure 43)

圖44

(2) 上動不停。兩腳蹬地向前跳起，空中左轉身90°，落步成偏馬步；同時，左拳變掌，從外向裏落於左胸前，掌心向右，掌指向上；右拳從外向內畫弧，拳心向下，拳面抵於左掌心；目視右方。（圖44、圖44附圖）

圖 44 附圖

(2) Don´t stop the above action, two feet jump up from the ground forward, the body turns 90° to the left in the air, change the fall step into the slanting horse stance. At the same time, change the left fist into palm, fall in front of the chest from the outside to inward, with the palm turning to the right, the fingers up. The right fist pulls an arc from the outside to inward, with the fist–palm down, and the fist–plane presses on the left palm. Eyes look rightward. (Figure 44, Attached figure 44)

圖 45

(3) 上動不停。身體略向右轉，重心右移成右弓步；同時，左掌推右拳向右前方頂肘，肘尖向右，高與肩平；目視右前方。（圖 45）

(3) Don´t stop the above action, the body turns to the right slightly. Shift the barycenter to the right to change into the bow stance. At the same time, the left palm pushes the right fist to strike right forward with the elbow, with elbow tip turning to the right, at the shoulder height. Eyes look right forward.〔Figure 45〕

圖 46

（4）上動不停。身體右轉 180°；左腳經右腳內側向前上一步，重心前移成左弓步；同時，隨轉身右拳變掌，右肘下落；左肘抬起，左掌變拳抵於右掌心，右手推左拳向前頂肘；目視左前方。（圖 46）

（4）Don´t stop the above action, the body turns 180° to the right. The left foot takes a step forward through the inner side of the right foot, shift the barycenter forward and change into the left bow stance. At the same time, change the right fist into palm with the rotation of the body, and the right elbow falls down; lift the left elbow, change the left palm into fist to press the right palm. The right hand push the left fist forward to strike with the elbow. Eyes look left forward.（Figure 46）

羅漢拳

圖 47

26. 獨龍出洞
Single dragon comes out of cave

　　接上勢。右腳經左腳內側向前上一步，重心前移成右弓步；同時，左拳變掌，經胸前向外摟，變拳抱於腰間，拳心向上；右掌自腰間向前穿掌，掌心向上，高與肩平；目視右掌。（圖47）

羅漢拳套路動作圖解

Follow the above posture, the right foot takes a step forward through the inner side of the left foot, shift the barycenter forward and become the right bow stance. At the same time, change the left fist into palm and grab outward through the front of the chest, then change it into the fist and hold it on the waist, with the fist–palm up; thread out the right palm forward from the waist, with the palm up, at the shoulder height. Eyes look at the right palm.（Figure 47）

圖 48

27. 追風炮
Cannon chasing the wind

接上勢。身體左轉 180°，右腳向左腳內側併步震腳；同時，左拳變掌，經胸前向外摟，變拳抱於腰間，拳心向上；右掌變拳，從右腰間向前沖拳，拳心向下，高與肩平；目視前方。（圖 48）

羅漢拳套路動作圖解

Follow the above posture, turn the body 180° to the left, bring the right foot together to the inner side of the left one. At the same time, change the left fist into palm and grab outward through the front of the chest, then change it into the fist and hold on the waist with the fist–palm up, change the right palm into fist and strike forward from the right side of the waist with the fist–palm down, at the shoulder height. Eyes look forward. (Figure 48)

圖 49

28. 臥枕
Rest on the pillow

　　接上勢。身體左轉 90°，兩腳同時跳起，向身體兩側落步，蹲身成右弓步；同時，右拳經胸前從下向上抄抱，置於右胸前，拳心向裏，拳面向上；左拳經胸前向下栽拳至襠前，拳眼向右；目視左方。（圖 49）

羅漢拳套路動作圖解

Follow the above posture, turn the body 90° to the left, jump up with the feet together, and land to the both sides of the body, squat the body into the right bow stance. Simultaneously lift the right fist upwards through the front of the chest from downward and place it in front of the right chest, with the fist–palm inward and the fist–plane up; punch the left fist downward to the front of the crotch through the front of the chest with the fist–hole rightward. Eyes look to the left. (Figure 49)

圖 50

29. 端槍式
Holding gun position

（1）接上勢。右拳變掌，在胸前向下、向左畫掌，隨即向外摟至右膝外側，掌指向前，掌心向下；同時，左拳變掌，附於右肘內側，掌指向右，掌心向下；兩腿成右弓步；目視右掌指。（圖50）

羅漢拳套路動作圖解

(1) Follow the above posture, change the fist into palm, pull the palm downward and leftward in front of the chest, then grab it outward to the outer side of the right knee with the fingers forward and the palm downward. Simultaneously, change the left fist into palm and press it to the interior of the right elbow with the palm fingers rightward and the palm downward. Both legs form a right bow stance. Eyes look the fingers of the right palm. (Figure 50)

圖 51

(2) 上動不停。身體左轉 90°；同時，右臂微屈，右掌變拳置於右胯處，拳心向外；左掌變拳護於胸前；目視右下方。（圖 51）

(2) Don´t stop the above action, turn the body 90° to the left. Simultaneously, slightly bend the right arm, change the right palm into fist and place it on the right hip with the fist–palm outward; the left palm changes into fist and guards round the chest Eyes look the right downward.（Figure 51）

圖 52

(3)上動不停。身體右轉 90°，左腿獨立，右腿提膝，腳尖內扣；同時，右拳屈臂上提，經胸前向前反砸，拳心向裏，高與頜平；左拳附於右肘內側，拳心向上；目視右拳。（圖52）

(3) Don´t stop the above action, turn the body 90° to the right, the left leg stands alone, raise the knee of the right leg and the tiptoe turns inward. Simultaneously, bend the arm to raise the right fist, pound forward through the front of the chest with the fist-palm inward at the chin height; press the left fist to the interior of the right elbow with the fist-palm up. Eyes look at the right fist.（Figure 52）

圖 53

30. 追蛇入洞
Chase the snake into cave

(1) 接上勢。右腳向前落地，身體下蹲成跪步；同時，右拳收回腰間，隨即再向前下方沖拳，拳心向下；左拳收回腰間，拳心向上；目視右拳。（圖 53）

羅漢拳套路動作圖解

(1) Follow the above posture, the right foot falls to the ground forward, and squat the body to the kneel stance. Simultaneously, draw back the right fist on the waist, then strike front downward with the fist–palm down; draw back the left fist on the waist with the fist–palm up. Eyes look at the right fist. (Figure 53)

羅
漢
拳

圖54

(2) 上動不停。左腳向前上步，仍成跪步；同時，右拳抱於腰間，拳心向上；左拳向前下方沖拳，拳面朝斜下方；目視左拳。（圖54）

(2)Don´t stop the above action, the left foot steps forward, and still keeps the kneel stance. Simultaneously, hold the right fist on the waist with the fist–palm up; the left fist strike ahead downward with the fist–plane downward aslant. Eyes look at the left fist.（Figure 54）

圖 55

31. 虎尾腳　Tiger-tail Foot

接上勢。身體提起，左腿獨立；同時，右腿向右後方踹出；目視右腳。（圖 55）

要點：左腿獨立，重心要穩固，右踹腿要高，力達腳跟。

Follow the above posture, raise the body with the left leg standing alone. Simultaneously, the right leg kicks toward the right backside. Eyes look at the right foot.（Figure 55）

Key points: when the left leg standing alone, keep the barycenter steady; the right leg kicks at a certain height with the force reaching the heel.

圖 56

32. 二起腳　Jumping kick twice

（1）接上勢。右腳向左腳內側落腳併步，身體下蹲成蹲步；同時，身體左轉，左拳抱於腰間，拳心向上；目視前方。（圖56）

(1) Follow the above posture, the right foot falls and bring together to the interior of the left one, squat the body to be the squat stance. Simultaneously, turn the body to the left, hold the left fist on the waist with the fist—palm up. Eyes look forward. （Figure 56）

圖 57

（2）上動不停。左腳屈膝跳起，右腿同時向上彈踢，膝蓋挺直，腳面繃緊；同時，右拳變掌，向前拍擊右腳面；目視右掌。（圖 57）

（2）Don´t stop the above action, bend the left knee to jump up, snap kick upward with the right leg, straightening the knee, tightening the instep. Simultaneously, change the right fist into palm, slap the right instep forward. Eyes look at the right palm. （Figure 57）

圖 58

33. 丁步亮掌　Flash palm in T-stance

(1)接上勢。身體左轉 90°，雙腿左右分開落地；同時，雙掌經腹前向左擺掌，右掌略低於左掌，兩掌心均向下，掌指向左；目視左方。（圖 58）

(1) Follow the above posture, turn the body 90° to the left, the two legs fall to the ground separately. Simultaneously, swing the two palms forward through the front of the abdomen, and the right palm shall be little lower than the left one, with two palms down, the fingers leftward. Eyes look leftward.〔Figure 58〕

圖 59

(2) 上動不停。左腳向右腳內側靠近，蹲身成左丁步；同時，兩手向上、向右畫掌，右掌立於身體右側，高與肩平；左臂屈肘，左掌立於右肩前，左掌略低於右掌；目視右掌。（圖59）

(2) Don´t stop the above action, put the left foot together to the interior of the right one, squat the body into the left T-stance. Simultaneously, pull palms upward and rightward. The right palm shall be in the right side of the body at shoulder levell, bend the left elbow, the left palm shall be little lower than the right one and in front of the right shoulder. Eyes look at the right palm.（Figure 59）

圖60

第三段　Section Three

34. 龍盤窩　Dragon entrenches on cave

（1）接上勢。左腳向左側開半步，重心左移；同時，右腿伸直，經身前向左、向後掃腿，右腿掃至左側時，上身前俯，兩手扶地；左腳隨即蹬地讓過右腿；目視右腳。（圖60）

羅
漢
拳
套
路
動
作
圖
解

(1) Follow the above posture, the left foot takes a half–step leftward, transfer the barycenter to the left. Simultaneously, straighten the right leg and sweep it leftward and backward through the front of the body. When the right leg being swept to the left side, pronate the upper body forward, support the ground with the hands; then the left foot presses on the ground to give way to the right one. Eyes look at the right foot. (Figure 60)

圖61

(2)上動不停。左腳在右腿前落地；同時，右腿繼續向後、向右掃腿，成右僕步；目視右腳尖。（圖61）

要點：掃腿時手和腳配合，協調一致，掃腿迅速，乾淨俐落。

羅漢拳套路動作圖解

(2) Don´t stop the above action, the left foot lands to the ground before the right leg. Simultaneously, the right leg continues to sweep backward and rightward to form the right crouch stance. Eyes look at the right tiptoes.（Figure 61）

Key points: harmonize the hands with the feet when sweeping the leg, which shall be quick and efficient.

圖 62

35. 仙人照鏡
Immortals looks into mirror

　　接上勢。身體提起，右腳經左腳前向左側跨一步，落於左腳外側，向下蹲身成歇步；同時，右臂屈肘，向上擺掌至左耳側，掌指向上，掌心向右，高與耳平；左臂屈肘，左掌托於右肘下，掌心向上，掌指向右；目視右方。（圖 62）

羅漢拳套路動作圖解

Follow the above posture, raise the body, the right foot strides a step leftward through the front of the left one, and lands to the outer side of the left foot, then squat the body into the rest stance; at the same time, bend the elbow of the right arm upward and swing the palm to the side of the left ear, with the fingers up and the palm rightward at the ear level; bend the left elbow, support the right elbow with the left palm up and the fingers rightward. Eyes look at the right side. (Figure 62)

圖 63

36. 迎面沙
Head-on　sands

(1) 接上勢。起身，左腳向左側橫跨一步；同時，右掌向下、向右、向上、向左畫一立圓，向左腳前方蓋抓，掌心向下，微離地面；左掌向外、向上畫一小圓，立於右胸前；兩腿成左弓步，身體前俯；目視右掌。（圖 63）

羅漢拳套路動作圖解

(1) Follow the above posture, the body stands up, the left foot takes a sidestep leftward. Simultaneously, the right palm pulls a upright circle downward, rightward, upward and leftward, grab to front of the left foot with the palm downward and from the ground slightly; the left palm pulls a small circle outward and upward, keep it erectly in front of the right chest. The legs shall be in left bow stance, and the body shall pronate forward. Eyes look at the right palm. (Figure 63)

羅漢拳

圖 64

(2)上動不停。右手從左腳處抓握變拳，向上擺至右側上方，隨即向左抖腕變掌，置於頭右前方，掌心向左；兩腿成馬步；目視左方。（圖 64）

要點：撒掌抖腕發力，動作幅度不宜過大，眼隨手走。

羅
漢
拳
套
路
動
作
圖
解

(2) Don't stop the above action, the right hand grabs in the left foot and changes into fist, swing it upward to the right top, then do wrist snap to the left and change it into palm, place it the right ahead of the head with the palm leftward. Both legs form the horse stance. Eyes look at the left side. (Figure 64)

Key points: when scattering the palm and do the wrist snap to send force, the larger extent of the action shall be not suitable, the eyes shall follow the hands.

圖 65

37. 分掌箭彈　Separate palms and thrust kick

（1）接上勢。身體左轉 90°，右腳向左腳內側上步，向下蹲身；同時，兩掌由胸前向上、向外畫掌，置於腰間，掌心向上，掌指向前；目視前方。（圖65）

(1) Follow the above posture, turn the body 90° to the left, step the right foot forward to the interior of the left one and squat downward. Simultaneously, two palms pull through the front of the chest upward and outward, place them on the waist with the palm up and the fingers forward. Eyes look forward. (Figure 65)

圖 66

(2) 上動不停。左腳蹬地跳起，隨即右腿伸直向前彈踢；目視右腳。（圖 66）

要點：蹲步時大腿接近水平；彈踢時腳面繃直，力達腳面。

(2) Don´t stop the above action, the left foot jumps off the ground, then straighten the right leg for snap kick forward. Eyes look at the right foot. (Figure 66)

Key points: the thigh in the squatting step shall be close to the level; straighten the instep when doing the snap kick, the force shall reach the instep.

圖 67

38. 雙龍出洞
Two dragons come out of the cave

接上勢。兩腳向下落地，右腳在前左腳在後，成
右弓步；同時，兩掌從腰間向前穿出，兩臂微屈，掌
心向上，高與肩平；目視前方。（圖 67）

Follow the above posture, the feet land down to the ground
with the right foot in front and the left one at back into the right
bow stance. Simultaneously, the two palms thread out forward
from the waist, bend the arms slightly with the palms up at the
shoulder level. Eyes look forward.（Figure 67）

圖 68

39. 坐蓮聽經
Listen to the sutra on the lotus seat

接上勢。身體左轉 270°，下蹲成歇步；同時，兩
掌由胸前向下、向外畫掌，隨即兩掌變為劍指，屈臂
於兩耳側，劍指相對，高與耳平；目視前方。（圖
68）

Follow the above posture, turn the body 270° to the left and
squat into the rest stance. Simultaneously, the two palms pull
through the front of the chest downward and outward, then
change the two palms into sword fingers, bend the arms to the
sides of ears with the sword fingers opposite at the ear height.
Eyes look forward.（Figure 68）

圖 69

40. 羅漢托天　Arhat holds the sky

接上勢。身體起立，兩腿伸直；同時，兩手劍指變掌，經胸前向下畫掌，隨即向外、向上擺架於頭頂，掌心向上，掌指相對；目視兩掌指。（圖 69）

Follow the above posture, the body stands up, straighten the legs. Simultaneously, change the sword fingers into palms and pull them downward, then do the palm parry over the head with the palms up and the fingers opposite. Eyes look at the fingers of the two palms.（Figure 69）

圖 70

41. 羅漢下山 Arhat goes down the hill

(1) 接上勢。左腳向左側鏟出成仆步；同時，右掌變拳抱於腰間；身體前俯，左掌經胸前向左腳砍掌，掌心向下，掌指向前；目視左掌。（圖 70）

(1) Follow the above posture, the left foot shovels leftward and changes into crouch stance. Simultaneously, change the right palm into fist and hold it on the waist; pronate the body forward, the left palm chops to the left foot through the front of the chest with the palm down and the fingers forward. Eyes look at the left palm. (Figure 70)

圖 71

(2) 上動不停。身體左轉 90°，重心前移成左弓步；同時，左掌自右膝外屈臂上架於頭前上方，掌心向上，掌指向右；目視前方。（圖 71）

(2) Don´t stop the above action, turn the body 90° to the left, transfer the barycenter forward into the left bow stance. Simultaneously, put up the left palm over the upper part in front of the head with the palm up and the fingers rightward. Eyes look forward.〔Figure 71〕

圖 72

42. 左右採腳　Slap left and right feet

(1) 接上勢。重心前移，左腿獨立，右腳蹬地向前彈踢；同時，左掌變拳抱於腰間；右拳變掌，向前拍擊右腳面；目視右腳。（圖 72）

(1) Follow the above posture, transfer the barycenter forward, the left leg stands alone, then the right foot kick forward. At the same time, change the left palm into fist and hold it on the waist; change the right fist into palm, slap the right instep forward. Eyes look at the right foot.（Figure 72）

圖 73

(2) 上動不停。右腳向前落地，隨即左腳向前彈踢；同時，右拳抱於腰間，左拳變掌拍擊左腳面；目視左腳。（圖 73）

(2) Don't stop the above action, the right foot lands forward to the ground, then the left foot kicks forward. At the same time, hold the right fist on the waist, change the left fist into palm to slap the left instep. Eyes look at the left foot.（Figure 73）

羅漢拳套路動作圖解

圖 74

43. 二起腳　Jumping kick twice

接上勢。左腿屈膝下落，在左腳尚未落地時，右腳向前迅速彈踢；同時，左掌變拳，收抱於腰間；右拳變掌，向前拍擊右腳面；目視右腳。（圖 74）

Follow the above posture, bend the left knee, before the left leg falls to ground, the right foot kicks forward quickly. At the same time, change the left palm into fist and draw it back on the waist; change the right fist into palm and slap the right instep forward. Eyes look at the right foot.（Figure 74）

圖 75

44. 雲頂　Cloud top

（1）接上勢。兩腳先後落地，右腳在左腳前；目視右掌。（圖75）

(1) Follow the above posture, the feet land to the ground sequentially with the right foot before the left one. Eyes look at the right palm.〔Figure 75〕

圖 76

（2）上動不停。左腳向右腳前上一步，身體右轉
90°，隨即右腳向左腳後插步，兩腿成交叉步；同時，
左拳變掌，經胸前雲托於頭頂，掌心向上，掌指向
右；右掌翻掌，屈臂上托，掌指向右；目視右掌。
（圖 76 ）

（2）Don´t stop the above action, step the left foot forward,
turn the body 90° to the right, then let the right foot insert a step
behind the left one, and the legs form a cross stance, At the same
time, change the left fist into palm and place it on head top
through the front of the chest with the palm up and the fingers
rightward; turn over the right palm, bend the arm to support
upward, the fingers rightward. Eyes look at the right palm.
（Figure 76 ）

圖 77

(3) 上動不停。身體右轉 270°；同時，兩掌掌心向上，在頭頂自右向左雲頂後，變拳收抱於腰間；目視前方。（圖 77）

要點：雲頂動作與轉體要密切配合，協調完成。

(3) Don't stop the above action, the body turn 270° to the right. At the same time, keep the palms upward on the head top from the right to the left behind the cloud crown, then change them into fists and draw them back on the waist. Eyes look forward.（Figure 77）

Key points: coordinate the cloud crown action with the body turn closely to finish this action.

圖 78

45. 七星 Seven star

接上勢。左腳向右腳靠近，腳尖點地，蹲身成左
丁步；同時，右拳向前平沖，拳心向下，拳眼向左，
高與肩平；左臂屈肘前撐，拳面抵於右肘內側，拳心
向下；目視右拳。（圖78）

Follow the above posture, put together the left foot to the
right one with the tiptoe on the ground, squat in left T-stance.
Simultaneously, punch the right fist horizontally, with the
fist-palm down and the palm hole leftward at the shoulder level;
bend the left elbow forward to support, the fist-plane presses on
the inner side of the right elbow with the fist-palm down. Eyes
look at the right fist. (Figure 78)

圖 79

46. 馬步單鞭
Single whip in horse stance

（1）接上勢。身體左轉 90°，左腳向左橫跨一步成馬步；同時，兩拳外旋，屈肘合於胸前並齊，拳心向裏，高與頷平；目視前方。（圖 79、圖 79 附圖）

羅漢拳套路動作圖解

圖 79 附圖

(1) Follow the above posture, turn the body 90° to the left, stride the left foot a step leftward and form the horse stance. At the same time, two fists turn outward and bend elbows to bring together before the chest with the palms inward at the chin level. Eyes look forward.（Figure 79, Attached figure 79）

羅漢拳

圖 80

(2) 上動不停。兩拳分別向身體兩側平沖，拳心均向下，拳眼均向前，高與肩平；目視左拳。（圖 80）

要點：兩臂抱拳、沖拳要連貫一致，沖拳快速，自然彈回，力達拳面。

羅漢拳套路動作圖解

(2) Don´t stop the above action, two fists punch horizontally toward the two sides of the body separately, with the fist–palm down, two fist–holes forward at the shoulder level. Eyes look at the left fist. (Figure 80)

Key points: hold the two fists, the straight punch shall be coherent, consistent and quick, naturally rebound, the force shall reach the fist–plane.

圖 81

第四段　Section Four

47. 攔腰雙撅
Grasp waist for double punches

（1）接上勢。身體右轉 90°，重心前移成右弓步；同時，兩拳變掌，右掌向胸前畫掌，隨即和左掌一起向右前方畫掌。右臂微屈，高與肩平，掌心向斜下方；左掌略低於右掌，掌心向右，掌指向前；目視右掌。（圖 81）

羅漢拳套路動作圖解

(1) Follow the above posture, the body turn 90° to the right, shift the barycenter forward and become the right bow stance. At the same time, change two fists into palms, the right palm pulls toward the front of chest, then quickly pull it toward the right ahead with left palm. Bend the right arm slightly at the shoulder level, with the palm down aslant; the left palm shall be lower than right one slightly, with the palm turning to the right and the fingers forward. Eyes look at the right palm. (Figure 81)

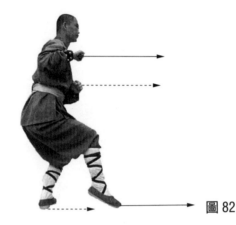

圖 82

(2) 上動不停。重心後移，右腳退半步，身體微蹲成右虛步；同時，兩掌抓握變拳，右拳屈臂收於右胸前，拳心向右下，左拳收於腹前，拳心向裏；目視前方。（圖 82）

(2) Don´t stop the above action, shift the barycenter back, the right foot takes a half-step back, the body squats slightly into the right empty stance. At the same time, two palms grab and change into fists, bend the right arm and draw back the right fist before the chest with the fist-palm toward the low right, draw back the left fist before the abdomen with the fist-palm inward. Eyes look forward.（Figure 82）

圖 83

（3）上動不停。右腳向前上一步，隨即左腳跟半步，成右弓步；同時，雙拳向前沖出，右拳高與肩平，拳眼向下，拳心向外；左拳略低於右拳，拳心向裏，拳眼向上；目視雙拳。（圖 83）

(3) Don´t stop the above action, the right foot takes a step forward, then the left foot follows a half–step and form a right bow stance. At the same time, the two fists punch forward, with the right fist at the shoulder level, the fist –hole down and the palm outward; the left fist is lower than right one slightly with the fist–palm inward and the fist–hole up. Eyes look at the two fists.（Figure 83）

羅漢拳

圖84

48. 小鬼提鞋
Ghost lifts shoe

(1) 接上勢。身體略右轉；同時，兩拳變掌，右掌向裏放於左手腕上，隨即兩掌翻絞成右掌在下，左掌在右手腕上；右掌掌心向上，掌指向前；左掌指斜向右方；目視前方。（圖84）

羅漢拳套路動作圖解

(1) Follow the above posture, the body turns to the right slightly. At the same time, change two fists into palms, the right palm turns inward and puts on the left wrist, then turn over two palms and make the right palm down and the left one on the right wrist. The right palm is up and the fingers is forward; the fingers of the left palm is rightward aslant. Eyes look forward. (Figure 84)

圖 85

（2）上動不停。身體右轉 90°，隨即左腳抬起，向左側上方踹腿；同時，右掌變拳收抱於腰間；左掌向左側橫推掌，掌心向下，掌指向右，高與肩平；目視左腳。（圖 85）

(2) Don´t stop the above action, the body turns 90° to the right, then lift the left foot and kick sideways toward the left ahead. At the same time, change the right palm into fist and hold on the waist; push horizontally the left palm leftward, with the palm down, the fingers rightward at the shoulder level. Eyes look at the left foot.（Figure 85）

羅漢拳套路動作圖解

圖 86

49. 窩心肘 Elbow toward the heart

接上勢。身體右轉 90°，左腳向前落地；同時，右臂屈肘向前斜擊，高與肩平；左掌外翻迎擊右肘，掌心向右，掌指向前；目視右肘。（圖 86）

Follow the above posture, the body turns 90° to the right, the left foot lands to the ground forward. At the same time, bend the elbow of the right arm and strike sideways forward at the shoulder level; the left palm turns outward and counterpunch the right elbow, with the palm rightward and the fingers forward. Eyes look at the right elbow.（Figure 86）

圖 87

50. 反背捶　Backhand hammer

接上勢。右拳自胸前向上、向前反背擊出，拳眼向右，拳背向前；目視右拳。（圖 87）

要點：發力迅速，力達拳背，右拳反砸後自然彈回。

羅漢拳套路動作圖解

Follow the above posture, turn over the right fist in front of the chest to strike upward and forward, with the fist-hole rightward and the back of the fist forward. Eyes look at the right fist. (Figure 87)

Key points: release the force quickly, and the force reaches the back of the fist, the right fist rebounds naturally after the back pounding.

圖 88

51. 連環五拳　Interlink　five　fists

（1）接上勢。右拳屈臂收回腰間，隨即向前平沖，拳心向下，高與肩平；同時，左掌變拳收抱於腰間；目視右拳。（圖88）

(1) Follow the above posture, bend the right arm and draw back the right fist on the waist, then thrust horizontally forward, with the fist－palm down at the shoulder level. At the same time, change the left palm into fist and hold on the waist. Eyes look at the right fist.（Figure 88）

羅漢拳套路動作圖解

圖 89

（2）上動不停。右拳收回抱於腰間；同時，左拳向前平沖，拳心向下，高與肩平；目視左拳。（圖 89）

(2) Don´t stop the above action, draw back the right fist and hold on the waist. At the same time, punch horizontally forward with the left fist, with the fist−palm down at the shoulder level. Eyes look at the left fist. (Figure 89)

圖 90

(3) 上動不停。左拳收回抱於腰間；同時，右拳向
前平沖，拳心向下，高與肩平；目視右拳。（圖 90）

(3) Don´t stop the above action, draw back the left fist and
hold on the waist. At the same time, thrust right fist horizontally
forward, with the fist–palm down at the shoulder level. Eyes
look at the right fist.〔Figure 90〕

圖 91

（4）上動不停。右腳向前上一步，身體下蹲成左跪步；同時，右拳收回抱於腰間；左拳向前下方沖拳；目視左拳。（圖91）

(4) Don´t stop the above action, the right foot takes a step forward, squat the body into the left kneel stance. At the same time, draw back the right fist and hold on the waist, the left fist strikes toward the down ahead. Eyes look at the left fist.（Figure 91）

圖 92

　　(5) 上動不停。左拳收回抱於腰間；同時，右拳向
前下方沖拳；目視右拳。（圖 92）

　　要點：沖拳要連貫迅速，一氣呵成。

　　(5) Don´t stop the above action, draw back the left fist and
hold on the waist. At the same time, the right fist strikes toward
the down ahead. Eyes look at the right fist.〔Figure 92〕

　　Key points: thrusting fist shall be coherent and quick
without any letup.

羅漢拳套路動作圖解

圖 93

52. 翻身連珠炮
Cannons in succession with turning-over

(1) 接上勢。身體左轉 270°成交叉步；同時，左拳經胸前直臂外擺於身體左側；右臂從外向上、向裏擺，屈臂置於胸前，拳心向裏，略低於肩；目視左方。（圖 93）

(1)Follow the above posture, the body turns 270° to the left and becomes the cross stance. At the same time, the left fist passes in front of the chest and swing the straight arm outward at the left side of the body, swing the right arm from outside to upward and inward, bend the arm and put it before the chest, with the fist-palm inward, lower than the shoulder slightly. Eyes look leftward. (Figure 93)

圖 94

(2) 上動不停。左腳向身體左側橫跨一步，身體下蹲成馬步；同時，右拳收抱於腰間；左拳屈臂向裏壓於左膝上方，拳心向裏；目視左拳。（圖 94）

(2) Don´t stop the above action, the left foot strides horizontally to the left side of the body, the body squats into the horse stance. At the same time, draw back the right fist and hold on the waist; bend the left arm inward and the left fist presses on the left knee, with the fist–palm inside. Eyes look at the left fist. （Figure 94）

羅漢拳套路動作圖解

圖 95

（3）上動不停。身體左轉 90°，右腳尖內扣，重心前移成左弓步；同時，左拳收抱於腰間；右拳自腰間向前沖拳，拳心向左成立拳，高與肩平；目視右拳。（圖 95）

(3) Don´t stop the above action, the body turns 90° to the left, the right tiptoe turns inward, shift the barycenter forward and form the left bow stance. At the same time, draw back the left fist and hold on the waist; the right fist strikes forward from the waist with the fist-palm leftward at the shoulder height. Eyes look at the right fist. (Figure 95)

羅漢拳

圖 96

(4) 上動不停。身體右轉 90°成馬步；同時，右拳收抱於腰間；左拳向身體左側沖拳，拳眼向上成立拳，高與肩平；目視左拳。（圖 96）

(4) Don´t stop the above action, the body turns 90° to the left and forms the horse stance. At the same time, draw back the right fist and hold on the waist; the left fist punches to the left side of the body with the fist–hole upward at the shoulder height. Eyes look at the left fist.（Figure 96）

圖 97

53. 回身兩拳 Turn body and punch twice

（1）接上勢。身體右轉 90°，左腳向右腳前上一步；同時，左拳收回抱於腰間；右拳立拳向前平沖，高與肩平；目視右拳。（圖 97）

（1）Follow the above posture, the body turns 90° to the right, the left foot takes a step to the front of the right one. At the same time, draw back the left fist and hold on the waist; strike the right fist horizontally forward with the fist–hole upward at the shoulder height. Eyes look at the right fist.（Figure 97）

羅漢拳

圖98

　(2) 上動不停。右拳收回抱於腰間；同時，左拳立
拳向前平沖，拳眼向上，高與肩平；目視左拳。（圖
98）

　(2) Don´t stop the above action, draw back the right fist and
hold on the waist.　At the same time,　strike the left palm
horizontally forward with the fist– plane upward at the shoulder
height. Eyes look at the left fist.（Figure 98）

圖 99

54. 羅漢步雲　Arhat steps on the cloud

接上勢。兩腳向前跳起，屈右臂向上挑拳，置於右耳側，拳心向後；同時，左拳變掌向下拍擊右前臂；目視前方。（圖99）

Follow the above posture, two feet jump up forward, bend the right arm and raise the fist upward, put it at the side of the right ear with the fist–palm backward. At the same time, change the left fist into palm to slap the lower part of the right arm downward. Eyes look forward.（Figure 99）

圖 100

55. 擊地炮
Ground cannon

（1）接上勢。兩腳向前落地，身體下蹲成蹲步；同時，左掌變拳，屈臂收於右肘關節內側；右拳向前下方沖拳；目視右拳。（圖 100）

羅
漢
拳
套
路
動
作
圖
解

(1) Follow the above posture, two feet lands to the ground forward, squat the body into the squat stance. At the same time, change the left palm into fist and draw it back at the inner side of right elbow joint with the left arm bended; the right fist strikes toward the lower front side. Eyes look at the right fist. (Figure 100)

圖 101

（2）上動不停。左拳向前下方沖拳；同時，右拳屈臂收於左肘關節內側；目視左拳。（圖 101）

(2) Don´t stop the above action, left fist punches toward the lower front side. At the same time, change right arm into fist and draw it back at the inner side of left elbow joint with the right arm bended. Eyes look at the left fist.（Figure 101）

圖 102

（3）上動不停。右拳向前下方沖拳；同時，左拳屈臂收於右肘關節內側；目視右拳。（圖 102）

要點：蹲步大腿成水平，兩拳抖肩發力，快速連貫。

(3) Don´t stop the above action, right fist strikes toward the lower front side. At the same time, bend left arm and draw back the left fist at the inner side of the right elbow joint. Eyes look at the right fist.〔Figure 102〕

Key points: in squatting, keep the thigh horizontal, do the shoulders snap with two fists to release force quickly and coherently.

圖 103

56. 雲頂
Cloud top

(1) 接上勢。身體起立，向右轉身 90°，左腳向身體左側橫跨一步；同時，左拳變掌，經胸前向上雲托於頭頂上方，掌心向上，掌指向右；右拳變掌，經胸前向右雲托於右側，掌心向上，高與耳平；目視右掌。（圖 103）

羅漢拳套路動作圖解

(1) Follow the above posture, the body stands up and turns 90° to the right, the left foot strides a step toward the left. At the same time, change the left fist into palm and hold forward above the head through the front of the chest with the palm up, the fingers rightward; change the right palm into palm and hold rightward at the right side through the front of the chest, with the palm up at the ear level. Eyes look at the right palm. (Figure 103)

圖 104

（2）上動不停。右腳向左腳外側倒一步，身體右轉270°，成高弓步；同時，兩手經頭頂繼續向左雲托，隨即變拳收抱於腰間；目視前方。（圖 104）

(2) Don´t stop the above action, the right foot takes a step toward the outer side of the left foot, the body turns 270° to the right and form the high bow stance. At the same time, two hands continue to hold leftward through the ahead, then change into the fist, draw back and hold on the waist respectively. Eyes look forward.〔Figure 104〕

羅漢拳套路動作圖解

圖 105

57. 七星　Seven star

接上勢。左腳向右腳靠近，腳尖點地，蹲身成左
丁步；同時，右拳向前平沖，拳心向下，拳眼向左，
高與肩平；左臂屈肘前撐，拳面抵於右肘內側，拳心
向下；目視右拳。（圖105）

Follow the above posture, put the left foot and the right one
together with the tiptoes on the ground, squat the body into the
left T-stance. At the same time, the right fist strikes horizontally
forward with the fist-palm down, the fist-hole turn leftward at
the shoulder height; bend elbow of the left arm and support
forward, the fist-plane props at the inner side of the right elbow
with the fist-palm down. Eyes look at the right fist. (Figure
105)

圖 106

58. 馬步單鞭　Single whip in horse stance

(1)接上勢。身體左轉 90°，左腳向左橫跨一步成馬步；同時，兩拳外旋，屈肘合於胸前併齊，拳心向裏，高與頜平；目視前方。（圖 106）

(1) Follow the above posture, the body turn 90° to the left, left foot strides a step leftward into a horse stance. At the same time, two fists rotate outward, bend the elbows and bring them together before the chest, with the fist-palm inward at the chin height. Eyes look forward.〔Figure 106〕

羅漢拳套路動作圖解

圖 107

（2）上動不停。兩拳分別向身體兩側平沖，拳心均向下，拳眼均向前，高與肩平；目視左拳。（圖107）

（2）Don´t stop the above action, two fists strike hori–zontally toward the two sides of the body respectively, with the fist–palm down, the fist–hole forward at the shoulder level. Eyes look at the left fist.（Figure 107）

圖 108

59. 二起腳　Jumping kick twice

（1）接上勢。身體左轉 90°，右腳向左腳內側上步成蹲步；同時，兩拳收抱於腰間；目視前方。（圖 108）

(1) Follow the above posture, the body turns 90° to the left, the right foot steps forward to the inner side of the left one and become the squat stance. At the same time, draw back two fists and hold them on the waist respectively. Eyes look forward. (Figure 108)

羅漢拳套路動作圖解

圖 109

(2) 上動不停。兩腳蹬地跳起，右腳隨即向上彈踢；同時，右拳變掌拍擊右腳面。（圖 109）

(2) Don´t stop the above action, two feet jump up from the ground, then the right foot kicks forward. At the same time, change the right fist into palm to slap the right instep. ﹝Figure 109﹞

圖 110

60. 五花坐山
Swing arms with horse stance

　　(1) 接上勢。左腳落地，身體右轉 90°，右腳在身
體右側震腳落地，隨即左腳提起，扣於右膝後；同
時，右掌變拳擺向身體右側，拳心向上；左拳自腰間
向上擺至頭頂，拳心向上，拳眼向前；目視右拳。
（圖 110）

羅漢拳套路動作圖解

(1) Follow the above posture, the left foot falls to the ground, the body turns 90° to the left, the right foot falls to the ground with stamping the foot at the right side of the body, then raise up the left foot, put it at the back of the right knee. At the same time, change the right palm into fist to swing toward the right side of the body with the fist–palm up; the left fist swing upward to the head top from the waist, with the fist–palm up, the fist–hole forward. Eyes look at the right fist. (Figure 110)

圖111

（2）上動不停。左腳向身體左側落步成馬步；同時，左拳經胸前向下栽拳，拳面頂於左膝蓋上，拳心向後；右拳內旋向上架於頭部前上方約 15 公分處，拳心向前，拳眼向下；發「威」聲，目視左方。（圖111）

(2) Don't stop the above action, left foot lands at the left side of the body and become the horse stance. At the same time, the left fist punches down through the front of the chest, the fist-plane withstands on the knee with the fist-palm backward; the right fist rotates inward and parryies forward over the 15cm place in front of the head, with the fist-palm forward, the fist-hole down. Sound the voice of "wei" eyes look leftward. (Figure 111)

羅漢拳套路動作圖解

圖 112

61. 收勢　Closing form

（1）接上勢。左腳向右成併步；同時，兩拳抱於腰間；目視左方。（圖 112）

(1) Follow the above posture, the left foot moves to the right and bring feet together. At the same time, two fists hold on the waist respectively. Eyes look leftward.（Figure 112）

羅漢拳

圖 113

　　(2) 上動不停。兩拳同時自然下垂於身體兩側；目視前方。（圖 113）

　　(2) Don´t stop the above action, two fists drop naturally at the two sides of the body. Eyes look forward.〔 Figure 113 〕

全套動作演示圖

全套動作演示圖
Demonstration of All the Action

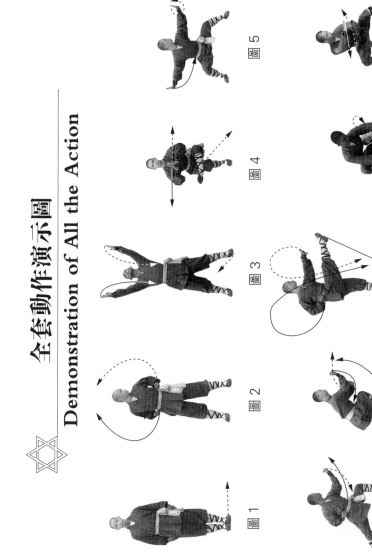

圖 1　圖 2　圖 3　圖 4　圖 5
圖 6　圖 7　圖 8　圖 9　圖 10

羅漢拳

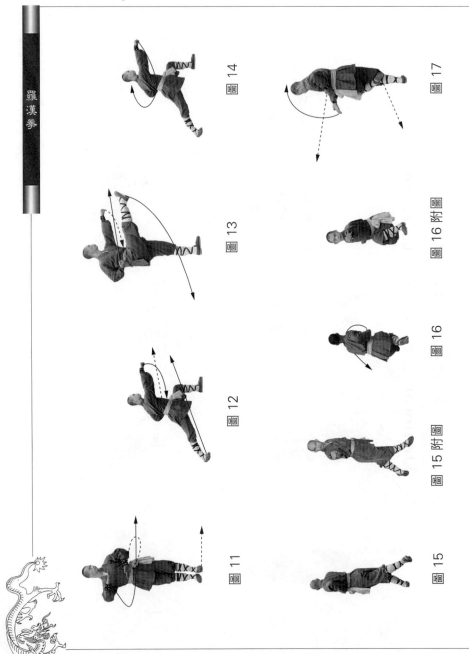

圖 14

圖 17

圖 13

圖 16 附圖

圖 12

圖 16

圖 15 附圖

圖 11

圖 15

图21

图20

图19

图18

图26

图25

图24

图23

图22

羅漢拳

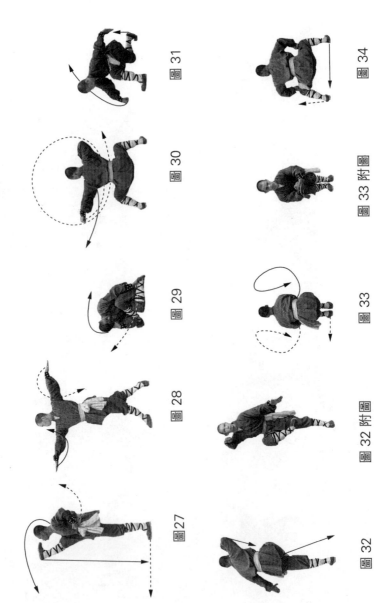

圖31
圖30
圖29
圖28
圖27

圖34
圖33 附圖
圖33
圖32 附圖
圖32

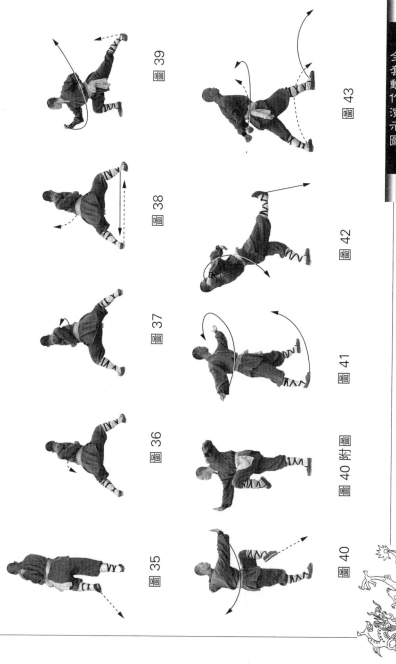

全套動作演示圖

圖 39

圖 38

圖 37

圖 36

圖 35

圖 43

圖 42

圖 41

圖 40 附

圖 40

羅漢拳

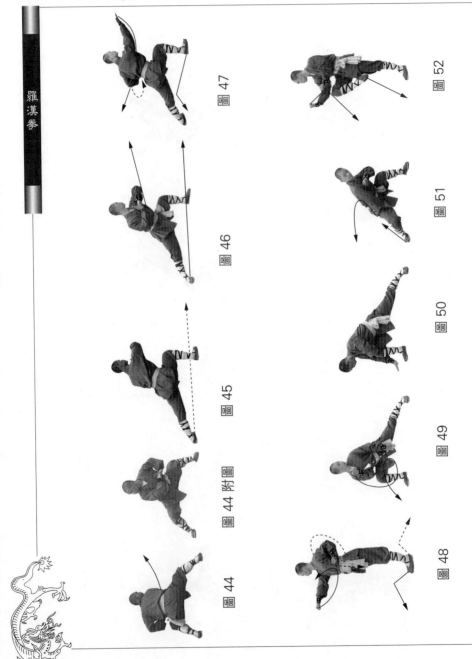

圖 44

圖 44 附圖

圖 45

圖 46

圖 47

圖 48

圖 49

圖 50

圖 51

圖 52

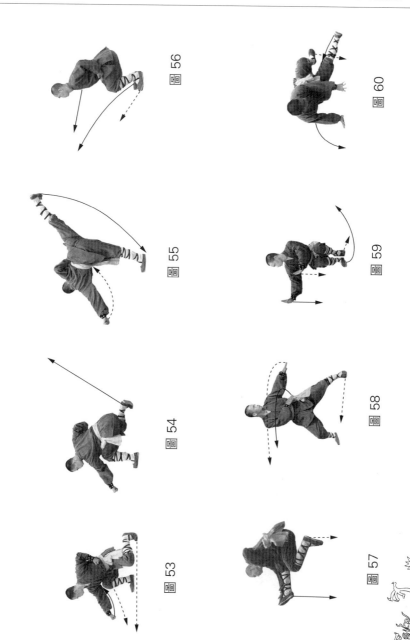

全套動作演示圖

圖 56

圖 60

圖 55

圖 59

圖 54

圖 58

圖 53

圖 57

羅漢拳

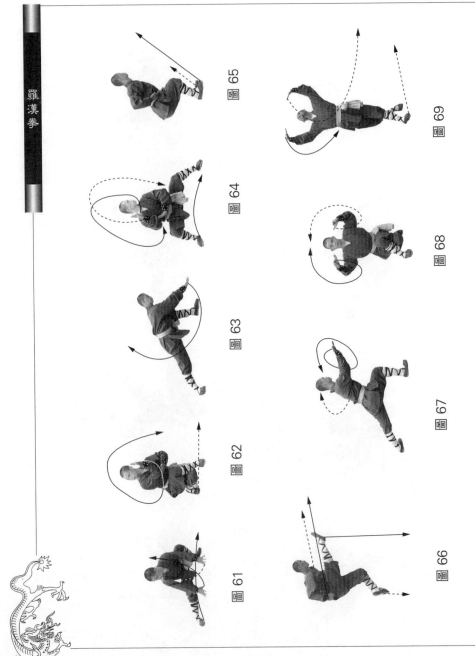

圖65

圖64

圖63

圖62

圖61

圖69

圖68

圖67

圖66

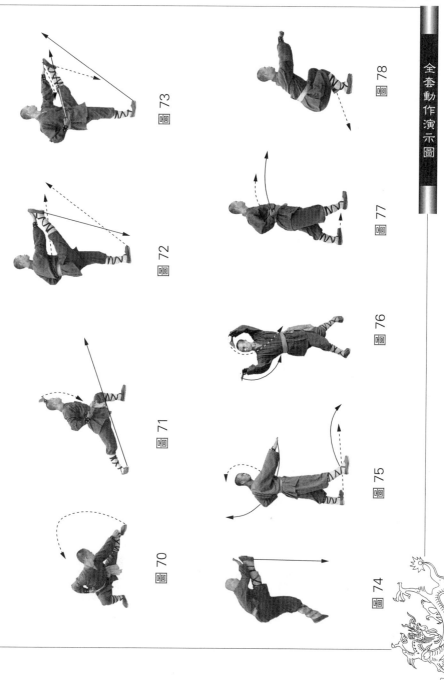

圖 73

圖 72

圖 71

圖 70

圖 78

圖 77

圖 76

圖 75

圖 74

羅漢拳

圖 79

圖 79 附圖

圖 80

圖 81

圖 82

圖 83

圖 84

圖 85

圖 86

圖 87

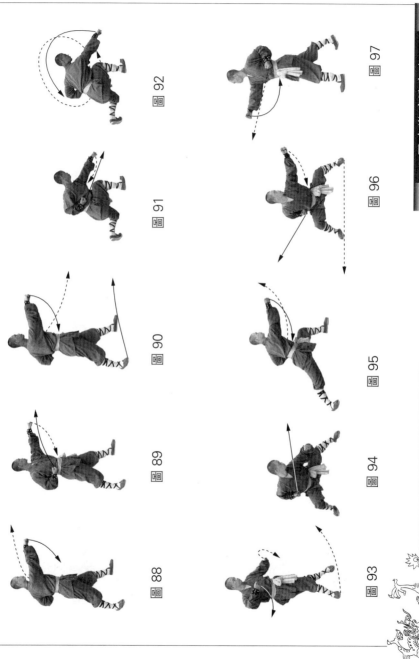

全套動作演示圖

羅漢拳

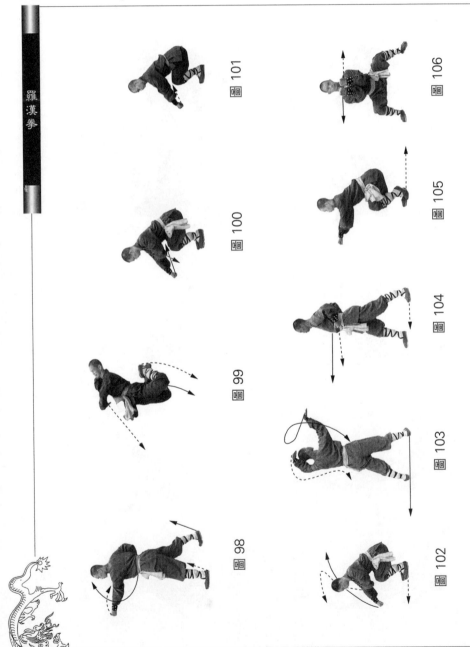

圖 98 圖 99 圖 100 圖 101

圖 102 圖 103 圖 104 圖 105 圖 106

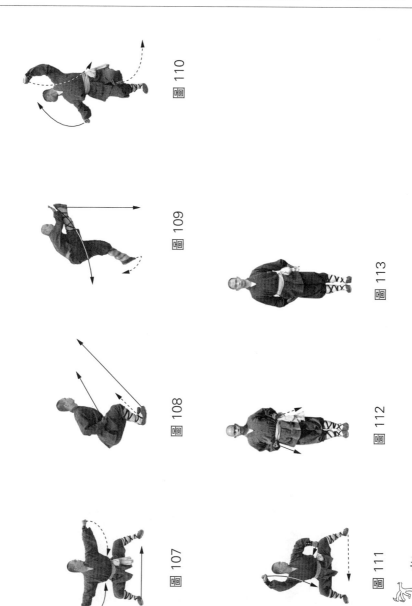

圖 110

圖 109

圖 113

圖 108

圖 112

圖 107

圖 111

全套動作演示圖

導引養生功

1 疏筋壯骨功＋VCD　定價350元

2 導引保健功＋VCD　定價350元

3 頤身九段錦＋VCD　定價350元

4 九九還童功＋VCD　定價350元

5 舒心平血功＋VCD　定價350元

6 益氣養肺功＋VCD　定價350元

7 養生太極扇＋VCD　定價350元

8 養生太極棒＋VCD　定價350元

9 導引養生形體詩韻＋VCD　定價350元

10 四十九式經絡動功＋VCD　定價350元

張廣德養生著作　每冊定價350元

全系列為彩色圖解附教學光碟

輕鬆學武術

1 二十四式太極拳＋VCD　定價250元

2 四十二式太極拳＋VCD　定價250元

3 八式十六式太極拳＋VCD　定價250元

4 三十二式太極劍＋VCD　定價280元

5 四十二式太極劍＋VCD　定價250元

彩色圖解太極武術

1 太極功夫扇

定價220元

2 武當太極劍
定價220元

3 楊式太極劍56式
定價220元

4 楊式太極刀
定價220元

5 二十四式太極拳+VCD

定價350元

6 三十二式太極劍+VCD

定價350元

7 四十二式太極劍+VCD
定價350元

8 四十二式太極拳+VCD

定價350元

9 楊式十六式太極劍
定價350元

10 楊氏二十八式太極拳+VCD

定價350元

11 楊式太極拳四十式+VCD

定價350元

12 陳式太極拳五十六式+VCD

定價350元

13 吳式太極拳五十六式+VCD
定價350元

14 精簡陳式太極拳八式十六式

定價220元

15 精簡吳式太極拳三十六式拳架·推手

定價220元

16 夕陽美功夫扇

定價220元

17 綜合四十八式太極拳+VCD
定價350元

18 三十二式太極拳四段

定價220元

19 楊式三十七式太極拳+VCD

定價350元

20 楊氏五十一式太極劍+VCD

定價350元

21 嫡傳楊家太極拳精練二十八式

定價220元

養生保健 古今養生保健法 強身健體增加身體免疫力

1 醫療養生氣功

醫療養生氣功
定價250元

2 中國氣功圖譜

中國氣功圖譜
定價250元

3 少林醫療氣功精粹

少林醫療氣功精粹
定價250元

4 龍形實用氣功

龍形實用氣功
定價220元

5 魚戲增視強身氣功

魚戲增視強身氣功
定價220元

7 道家玄牝氣功

道家玄牝氣功
定價200元

8 仙家秘傳袪病功

仙家秘傳袪病功
定價160元

9 少林十大健身功

少林十大健身功
定價180元

10 中國自控氣功

中國自控氣功
定價250元

11 醫療防癌氣功

醫療防癌氣功
定價250元

12 醫療強身氣功

醫療強身氣功
定價250元

13 醫療點穴氣功

醫療點穴氣功
定價250元

14 中國八卦如意功

中國八卦如意功
定價180元

15 正宗馬禮堂養氣功

正宗馬禮堂養氣功
定價420元

16 秘傳道家筋經內丹功

秘傳道家筋經內丹功
定價300元

17 三元開慧功

三元開慧功
定價250元

18 防癌治癌新氣功

防癌治癌新氣功
定價180元

19 禪定與佛家氣功修煉

禪定與佛家氣功修煉
定價200元

20 顛倒之術

顛倒之術
定價360元

21 簡明氣功辭典

簡明氣功辭典
定價360元

22 八卦三合功

八卦三合功
定價230元

23 朱砂掌健身養生功

朱砂掌健身養生功
定價250元

24 抗老功

抗老功
定價230元

25 意氣按穴排濁自療法

意氣按穴排濁自療法
定價250元

27 健身袪病小功法

健身袪病小功法
定價200元

28 張氏太極混元功

張氏太極混元功
定價250元

29 中國璇密功

中國璇密功
定價250元

30 中國少林禪密功

中國少林禪密功
定價200元

31 郭林新氣功

郭林新氣功
定價400元

32 八卦之源與健身養生

八卦之源與健身養生
定價280元

33 現代原始氣功1

現代原始氣功1
定價400元

34 養生開脈太極

養生開脈太極
定價300元

35 通靈功－養生袪病及入門功法

定價300元

太極跤

1 太極防身術
定價300元

2 擒拿術
定價280元

3 中國式摔角
定價350元

簡化太極拳

1 陳式太極拳十三式
定價200元

2 楊式太極拳十三式
定價200元

3 吳式太極拳十三式
定價200元

4 武式太極拳十三式
定價200元

5 孫式太極拳十三式
定價200元

6 趙堡太極拳十三式
定價200元

原地太極拳

1 原地綜合太極二十四式
定價220元

2 原地活步太極四十二式
定價200元

3 原地簡化太極拳二十四式
定價200元

4 原地太極拳十二式
定價200元

5 原地青少年太極拳二十二式
定價220元

6 原地兒童太極拳十捶十六式
定價180元

健康加油站

運動精進叢書

1 怎樣跑得快
定價200元

2 怎樣投得遠
定價180元

3 怎樣跳得遠
定價180元

4 怎樣跳的高
定價180元

5 高爾夫揮桿原理
定價220元

6 網球技巧圖解
定價220元

7 排球技巧圖解
定價230元

8 沙灘排球技巧圖解
定價230元

9 撞球技巧圖解
定價230元

10 籃球技巧圖解
定價220元

11 足球技巧圖解
定價230元

12 羽毛球技巧圖解
定價220元

13 乒乓球技巧圖解
定價220元

14 曲線球與飛碟球
定價300元

15 街頭花式籃球
定價280元

16 精彩高爾夫
定價330元

17 巴西青少年足球訓練方法
定價230元

國家圖書館出版品預行編目資料

羅漢拳＝Arhat Boxing／耿　軍　著
　　　——初版，——臺北市，大展，2008〔民97・02〕
　　　面；21公分，——（少林傳統功夫漢英對照系列；9）
　　　ISBN　978－957－468－588－2（平裝）

1.拳術　2.中國

528.97　　　　　　　　　　　　　　　　　　96024052

羅　漢　拳

ISBN 978－957－468－588－2

著　　者／耿　　軍
責任編輯／朱　曉　峰
發 行 人／蔡　森　明
出 版 者／大展出版社有限公司
社　　址／台北市北投區（石牌）致遠一路2段12巷1號
電　　話／（02）28236031・28236033・28233123
傳　　眞／（02）28272069
郵政劃撥／01669551
網　　址／www.dah-jaan.com.tw
E - mail ／service@dah-jaan.com.tw
登 記 證／局版臺業字第2171號
承 印 者／傳興印刷有限公司
裝　　訂／建鑫裝訂有限公司
排 版 者／弘益電腦排版有限公司
授 權 者／北京人民體育出版社
初版1刷／2008年（民97年）2月

定　價／200元

大展好書　好書大展
品嘗好書　冠群可期